CW00553101

AROUND
SEATON AND SIDMOUTH
IN OLD PHOTOGRAPHS

SAMUEL GOOD, SEATON'S FIRST PHOTOGRAPHER, c. 1869. Samuel Good was born at Seaton on 18 May 1827, the son of Joseph and Elizabeth Good. He first set up in business as a watchmaker and jeweller in Trinity Square, Axminster. Good was very keen on photography and when he moved back to premises in Fore Street, Seaton made this interest the second part of his business. Photography must have made a tremendous impact upon the Victorians and the early photographers were all professionals. Good, apart from recording events and scenes of local interest, also took many portraits, first using the Daguerrotype process, and later producing cartes-de-visite, the first cheap method enabling ordinary people to have their pictures taken.

AROUND
SEATON AND SIDMOUTH
IN OLD PHOTOGRAPHS

COLLECTED BY
TED GOSLING

ALAN SUTTON

Alan Sutton Publishing Limited
Phoenix Mill · Far Thrupp · Stroud · Gloucestershire

First published 1991

British Library Cataloguing in Publication Data

Around Seaton and Sidmouth in old photographs.
I. Gosling, Ted
942.357

ISBN 0-86299-949-9

Dedicated to my grandsons
Kane Edward and Oak

Typeset in 9/10 Korinna.
Typesetting and origination by
Alan Sutton Publishing Limited.
Printed in Great Britain by
The Bath Press, Avon.

CONTENTS

TAR SPRAYING BY THE KING'S ARMS, SEATON, 1934.

INTRODUCTION

The area covered by this book is bounded to the south by the waters of the English Channel and extends up to five miles inland. The main access road to the area is the A3052. This road follows a line first forged in pre-Roman times between Dorchester and Exeter. It is called Harepath at its closest point to Seaton, thought to derive from the Old English *herr path* or 'warrior's way'. Between the towns of Sidmouth, Seaton and Colyton are many small villages. Some are of only local importance but Beer, a small fishing village sheltered by the chalk cliff of Beer Head, is famed as the haunt of Jack Rattenbury, the notable Devon smuggler. Colyford, an ancient borough, has seen greater glory in earlier days.

For many centuries the economy of the area was based on the twin pillars of fishing and agriculture. Supplementing these were quarrying for the famed Beer limestone, used in Exeter Cathedral and other major buildings throughout southern England, and the small scale production of beautiful Honiton lace, worked by the women in most of the villages in the area.

Economic priorities started to change in the early nineteenth century when an interest was displayed by the wealthier classes in the supposed physical and medical benefits of sea-water bathing. This was first popularized by George III with his visits to Weymouth. When travel abroad became restricted due to the Napoleonic wars, many coastal towns on the south coast, with their mildness of winter climate, came to be favoured as resorts. Sidmouth was quick to take up this new role and much of its early nineteenth-century character still exists today.

With the arrival of the steam railway in the west of England in the mid-nineteenth century and the later extensions of single track lines to Sidmouth and Seaton, the basis of the local economy changed more quickly. Seaton developed as a resort much later than Sidmouth, but when its branch line was finished in 1868 Seaton and the attractive neighbouring coastal towns and villages were opened up to the new breed of adventurer – the relatively well-off Victorian holiday-maker. Very soon, new shops, hotels, boarding houses and bathing facilities were provided to take advantage of the new sources of income. Despite the boost which a wedding dress made of Honiton lace for Queen Victoria provided, the production of lace began to decline, due partly to the advent of machine-made net. Fishing continued to be important for many years, particularly at Beer, but now appears as only a shadow of its grand past. Axmouth harbour was of some importance in the mid-nineteenth century when two trading vessels sailed regularly to and from London and when coal, timber and quarrystone yards lined the Axe. But when a gale swept away the pier that had been built by John Hallett Esq., and then the railway reached Seaton, the marine trading life of the Axe ended for ever.

We are fortunate that the great expansion of the area coincided with the discovery of photography. Many Victorians were quickly attracted to this new art and photographs abounded, including posed portraits, buildings and views. Inevitably, the majority of these photographs are now lost. Most of us tend to be casual about the treatment of our immediate history but, fortunately, there are men around like Ted Gosling who have an overwhelming interest in their local area and a strong desire to keep a record of its past.

Ted is a Seatonian born and bred but the Seaton he remembers was a smaller, more closely knit community, where everyone was known to everyone else. His interest in local history and his accumulation of photographs and items of local interest started when he was a young man. He was soon organizing exhibitions of his collection in the local towns and villages, and has now become an authority on the local area. For a time, he was Honorary Curator of Lyme Regis Museum and, more recently, joined other like-minded people to form a museum in Seaton. This was successfully started three years ago and Ted is now Honorary Curator, and Secretary of the Axe Valley Heritage Association. The museum displays are based, to a large extent, around his collection of artefacts and photographs. The photographs offer an unparalleled view of the people and places of this area from the early days of photography to the recent past.

I am always grateful to those people with the vision to do the things that I always meant to do myself, such as preserving the reminders of the past while they are still available. Now we can all gain the benefit from that foresight, in the compelling pictures in this book. History is made more absorbing when there is a visual impact and these pictures will be of interest to all, whether they are familiar with the area or not.

Geoff Marshall
Mayor of Colyford, 1988 to 1991

The Towns

SIDMOUTH FROM SALCOMBE BRIDGE, 1875.

SEATON FRONT, c. 1855. This photograph is the oldest known of Seaton and was taken by Samuel Good, the town's first photographer. On the right of the foreground is an open space (now occupied by Esplanade properties) which was Mr Head's coal yard and it was here that the coal barges left their cargo. Castle and Cliff Houses were built by Samuel's father, Joseph Good, and he gave the land to the local authorities to enable them to build Castle Hill. The uninterrupted view of fields shows Cedric House as a sentinel in the background.

THE MILL DAM AND WEIR, SIDMOUTH, C. 1864. The mill dam, built in 1801, was washed away and replaced with a new dam in 1884.

SIDMOUTH FROM SALCOMBE HILL, C. 1875.

FORE STREET, SEATON, c. 1865. This photograph, taken by Samuel Good, shows the top end of Fore Street. The building on the left, with the tower, is the Sir Walter Trevelyan School. Designed by Benjamin Woodward, it was built in 1860. The school was greatly remodelled in the 1960s and has lost all but one of its original lancet windows. The tower over the entrance has been reduced in height.

LOOKING UP FORE STREET, SEATON, c. 1870. The row of houses in the foreground was named Violet Terrace; they are now the site of Windsor Gardens. This photograph was taken before the Town Hall was built. Also shown is a building with pillars and the figure of a lion over the door. This was the well-known pub called the Golden Lion, scene of much disorderly conduct during the Victorian era.

END OF WEST WALK, SEATON, August 1877. Showing Westcliff Terrace in the background, this picture was taken at least forty years before the Chine was built. The two pillars in the foreground mark a rear entrance to Check House, or Calverley Lodge as it was then called. Calverley Lodge was built by Joseph Good to the design of architect Benjamin Woodward for Sir Walter Calverley and Lady Trevelyan. The house cost £3,980 12s. 5d. to build, and with the manor of Seaton in the Trevelyan Estate, Calverley Lodge was used by the family as a summer residence.

SEATON BATH HOUSE AND THE ESPLANADE, July 1874. With the opening of the railway in 1868, Seaton changed from an isolated village to a seaside town. The Royal Clarence Hotel, standing on the left of this photograph, had just been built, the town was lit by gas, shops were increasing, and the Bath House, seen here in the centre, provided the residents and visitors alike with hot and cold sea-water baths.

HIGHWELL ROAD, SEATON, c. 1914. Highwell Road was built by James Leyman.

LOOKING DOWN SIDMOUTH STREET, now Harepath Road, Seaton, c. 1910. The old infants' school on the right of the foreground was built in 1840 by a Captain Proby, but at the time of this picture the building was used as the Manor Estate Office.

AXE BRIDGE, C. 1895. The house in the background, named Haven Cliff, was the residence of Colonel Hallett; he was descended from John Hallett, Lord of Axmouth Manor. John Hallett constructed the harbour at the mouth of the River Axe in 1850, which was capable of admitting ships of 150 tons burthen. Colonel Hallett, a fine horseman, was a familiar sight at that time, driving a four-in-hand.

HOUSES IN HARBOUR ROAD, SEATON, 1904. Harbour Road was called Cawsay Lane in 1609, Passageway in 1702 and became Station Road in 1868. After the station closed it was given its present name of Harbour Road. It formed part of the great medieval trackway that ran through the south of England.

GENERAL VIEW OF COLYTON FROM KINGSDOWN HILL, c. 1890.

THATCHED COTTAGES AT COLYTON, 1887. There is something cosy about a thatched roof; it seems to wrap a house round like a blanket and speaks of warmth and comfort. The thatched cottages in the towns and villages of East Devon are charming, and a subject for any artist.

MARKET PLACE, COLYTON, C. 1864. The Shambles, or Market House, which stood on the site of the present Feoffee's Hall, can be seen. The Market House, which housed the fire engine, had a large copper in one corner where soup was made, under the supervision of the Feoffees, during the winter months. Behind it was the old Red Lion Inn, a rendezvous for the supporters of the Duke of Monmouth. Across the road stood the Dolphin Hotel and posting yard. When this hotel was demolished the porch with pillars was moved to the Old Swan Inn, Colyford.

INTERIOR OF ST ANDREW'S CHURCH, COLYTON, August 1877.

SEA HILL, SEATON, 1926. The wall you can see on the right was the boundary wall of Seafield House, destroyed by enemy action in the Second World War.

THE ESPLANADE, SEATON, LOOKING WEST, c. 1925. The attractive building on the right of the foreground was the Westleigh Hotel. Built before the First World War by George Henry Richards, the Westleigh was one of eight hotels in the town; all have now ceased trading. The house standing in the present Jubilee Gardens was called Seafield; this was destroyed by a German bomber in the Second World War.

FRED DIMENT'S GARAGE, STATION ROAD, SEATON, C. 1908. Diment opened the first garage in Seaton in 1905. The premises were in Station Road (now Harbour Road) and he was the agent for Sunbeam and Star cars. The business was bought in 1908 by Ben Trevett, who lived with his family in the adjoining house. His son George took over the garage in 1936 and ran the business until his retirement in 1978. George Trevett, who died in 1985, was involved in many of the sporting activities of the town.

THE GEORGE INN, SEATON, C. 1885. This photograph shows a smaller George Inn than we know today. It was then situated between the Wilts and Dorset Bank, whose branch was on the corner of Fore Street, and the old Cornwall Bank, where the lounge bar is to be found today.

OLD SEATON, 1855. Taken before the Royal Clarence was built, this picture would have looked very much like the place that Polwhele described towards the end of the nineteenth century as a 'remarkably neat village in which every house has a finished air.' Although Fore Street is recognizable, the thatched cottages in the foreground have all been demolished.

FORE STREET, SEATON, 1884. The shop on the right belonged to Albert Gowen, who owned the first family and dispensing chemists shop in Seaton. He was licensed to sell methylated spirits and also ran a circulating library from his premises. This shop passed from Gowen to a Mr Gosney, then became Hinton Lake, and is today the premises of the Byrne-Jones family.

OLD BEER ROAD, SEATON, August, 1877.

THE OLD FERRY, RIVER AXE, SEATON, C. 1877. This photograph was taken four months after the opening of the concrete bridge over the River Axe. Before the new bridge was opened, travellers to and from Axmouth had to cross in a ferry boat, which in later years was worked by an overhead cable system. The ferryman lived in the first small house on the left next to the warehouse. At the mouth of the river the old custom house can be seen; this was washed away during the gales of January 1915.

THE MILL DAM, SIDMOUTH, showing the entrance to the mill leat, c. 1875. The mill dam was built in 1801 to feed a leat which took water down under Salcombe Road to Hooks Mill. This mill ground flour, and the splash of water with the turning of the wheel was one of the delights of early Sidmouth.

LOOKING WEST FROM THE SIDMOUTH ESPLANADE, c. 1890. You can see the cliff of Peak Hill in the background, standing 526 ft above mean sea level and looking very impressive. The Esplanade, built in 1837 at a cost of around £2,000, was replaced by the present one in 1926. Severe storms during previous winters caused much damage, demolishing sections and allowing the sea to flood the town.

THORNFIELD, SEATON, c. 1918. At the time of this picture Thornfield was the residence of Edward Cazelet Meade Esq.

LOOKING UP HAREPATH ROAD, SEATON, c. 1910. The town finished at the junction of Seaton Down Road with Harepath Road, and the Manor Cottages on the right, built in 1901, were the last houses in Seaton. You can see the council yard in the background, standing where Circle K now operate.

WESTLEIGH PRIVATE HOTEL, SEATON, C. 1925. At the time of this picture, the hotel was under the personal supervision of the proprietress, a Mrs Wallace. The hotel was open all the year, and the Westleigh was an ideal winter residence, having heated corridors and fires in all rooms. On the opposite side of The Square, now the site of Woolworths, was Goulds Temperance Hotel and Restaurant.

TREVETT'S CAR PARK, SEATON, C. 1962. This car park, now the site of Fosseway Court in Harbour Road, was built on the Burrow in 1936.

THE MILL FORD, SIDMOUTH, C. 1865. Milford Road, following the east bank of the Sid upstream to Waterloo Bridge and the toll-house, can be seen. The bridge was built in 1817, providing a more convenient connection between Sidmouth and Salcombe Regis, and the toll-house and gate were erected to pay for the new road. This photograph would have been taken over forty years before Milford Terrace was built.

SIDMOUTH. SIDBURY FROM THE HARCOMBE ROAD, C. 1865.

MAJOR TERRACE, SEATON, c. 1895.

LOOKING UP QUEEN STREET, SEATON, c. 1924. At the time of this photograph S. Lock Esq. had a bakers and confectionery business in the corner building now occupied by the George Inn. He also provided teas and light refreshments, and made wedding and birthday cakes which cost from 5s. to 5 gn. On the opposite side of The Square, Abbotts sold fancy gifts, tobacco, high class stationery and toys, and were the sole agents for Foley China.

FORE STREET, SIDMOUTH. This picture shows premises in Fore Street occupied by E. Culverwell and Sons. The family was famous for its long association with the *Sidmouth Herald*, spanning many generations. The newspaper was first published as *Harvey's Sidmouth Directory* in 1849. When the Culverwell family owned it the title had changed to the *Sidmouth Directory and General Advertiser*. The building was formerly known as the Herald Office, and the town centre premises are now a Lewis Meeson newsagent's shop.

AERIAL VIEW OF SEATON, c. 1931. This photograph shows plainly that the development of the town had started to take place. New houses were being built in Meadow Road, shown in the background, although work in Havenview Road had not yet started. Although Townsend Road had been constructed, building had not commenced. The Town Hall can be clearly seen in the background on the right hand side of the photograph; the row of houses running opposite was called Violet Terrace; it is now Windsor Gardens. Work on the Orchard had started and one can see the new bowling greens and the tennis courts which had been completed in 1928. The large white building standing on the front was the Cliff House Hotel, owned by the Good family. Seafield House can also be seen, but this was later destroyed by a German bomber in the Second World War.

DEMOLITION OF ONE OF SEATON'S OLDEST HOUSES, which stood at the junction of Beer Road and Queen Street. This property was knocked down in the 1960s to improve the corner.

CROSS STREET, SEATON, C. 1972. The row of houses on the left was known as Violet Terrace and was demolished in the early 1970s. This made way for the present Windsor Gardens.

LOOKING DOWN FORE STREET, SEATON, TOWARDS THE SEA, C. 1875. The house on the left with the pillars and gas lamp is Netherhayes, then the residence of Doctor Evans. In the background, one can catch a glimpse of the barges that used to unload coal on Seaton beach.

QUEEN STREET, SEATON, top of Manor Road, c. 1904. The imposing building to the left was once known as Brick House. It got its name because, when built in 1824, it was one of the first houses in the town constructed with brick. During the 1890s it became the Friendenhelm Seaside School for Girls, but by the time of this photograph was called Montpellier School. Later still it became Ferris and Prescott's the drapers, and at the present time a part of the building is used by Barclays Bank.

WESTCLIFF TERRACE, SEATON, C. 1875. This picture, looking west, gives a clear view of Westcliff Terrace long before the Chine was built. At this time, four out of eight residences in Westcliff Terrace were apartment houses.

MITCHELL TURNER & CO had wine vaults in Prospect House when this picture was taken of Fore Street, Seaton in September 1877. The iron railing on the right was in front of a house built by John Head and is now the Midland Bank.

GENERAL VIEW OF OLD BEER ROAD AND SEATON, c. 1901.

THIS IS HOW QUEEN STREET LOOKED at its junction with Beer Road and Cross Street in 1899. You can see by the lamp standard in the foreground that street lighting was provided by the Seaton Gas and Coke Company. Behind the house where the post office now stands was situated a coal yard run by the Badcock family. Fred Cockram's fishmongers was then a private residence, occupied by a solicitor.

LOOKING UP SIDMOUTH STREET, SEATON, c. 1902. The spire of the Mission Church of the Good Shepherd can be seen at the top right of this photograph. This church, erected at a cost of £1,250 in 1889, was sold in the 1970s and became the offices of John Wood. The house on the left with the notice board, standing on what is now the site of The Sweet Shop, belonged to Mrs Richards, who sold refreshments, sweets and newspapers.

VIOLET TERRACE, SEATON, 1895.

TREVELYAN ROAD, SEATON, c. 1910. Among the most attractive and solid looking houses in Seaton are those on the harbour side of Trevelyan Road, pictured here. When these properties were being built in 1906, labourers on the site were paid 3½d. an hour. Craftsmen were paid 6d. and they worked from 6.30 a.m. until 6 p.m. with only a break for lunch.

COUNCIL COTTAGES, SEATON, c. 1912.

SUMMERLAND PLACE, SEATON, c. 1905.

LOOKING DOWN FORE STREET, SEATON, c. 1904. The thatched cottages on the right of the foreground stood next to the old Seaton Primary School and were pulled down in recent years. At the time of this photograph they were occupied by Mr W.H. Aplin, who ran the Manor Farm Dairy. Behind the iron railings on the right was a paddock, where Sidney Boalch, the well-known local butcher, kept fowls. This is now the site of St Clare's.

ST ANDREW'S CHURCH, COLYTON, 1877. The base of the imposing tower of this church is thirteenth century, while the top is fourteenth century. The noted Devon antiquary Sir William Pole was buried in the chancel in 1635, and a tablet in the church tells of the Commonwealth vicar John Wilkins who was ejected at the Restoration.

THE RIVER COLY and the bottom of Dolphin Street, Colyton, April 1877.

THE ROYAL CLARENCE HOTEL, SEATON c. 1895. Built in 1866, the Royal Clarence was for many years a private concern run by the well-known Adams family but, by the time this photograph was taken, the business had merged with the Beach House into a limited company. The manageress was Miss Plimsole and the company directors were Mr A. Oakley of the Grove, Mr Yapp, a solicitor, and Mr Toms of Mitchell and Toms, the Chard brewery. The Royal Clarence was a first class hotel, with spacious dining, drawing, coffee and billiard rooms.

MARINE PLACE, SEATON, c. 1924. The drinking fountain to the right of the foreground was given to the town by Mr Willans to mark the Diamond Jubilee of Queen Victoria in 1897. Local children were forbidden by their parents to drink from the fountain in case they contracted some terrible disease.

FORTFIELD TERRACE, SIDMOUTH. This terrace was constructed in 1795 on the west side of town to face the sea. The Fort Field in front of the terrace and other open spaces contribute to the charm of present-day Sidmouth. This photograph, taken in 1865, shows Fortfield Terrace before the balconies were added and the whole terrace faced.

A LATER VIEW OF FORTFIELD TERRACE, C. 1880. The balconies have now been added and the terrace rendered. Fortfield Terrace has had some important tenants in its time, including the Grand Duchess Helena, sister-in-law to the Czar of Russia, who stayed in No. 8 Fortfield. Her visit is commemorated by the double-headed eagle in the pediment of the terrace.

THE ESPLANADE HOTEL, SEATON, was open for luncheons, teas and other refreshments when this picture was taken in 1925. The premises are now occupied by the Trustee Savings Bank. The charabanc on the right belonged to C.R. Good of the Pioneer Garage, Beer, whose buses at this time met all the trains at Seaton station.

SEATON, WEST WALK, c. 1926. Pictured here just after completion, the West Walk added to the attractions of the town.

THE NEW WEST WALK, SEATON, C. 1926. Seaton at this time was a typical middle-class seaside town, genteel in the summer and desolate in the winter. The few holiday-makers who were lucky enough to be able to afford to get away, would promenade up and down the front when the sun shone, or doze in hired deck-chairs while their children paddled in the sea or made sand-castles.

LOVERS LANE, SEATON, C. 1904. This quiet, tree-lined lane, favoured by courting couples at the turn of the century, is now Marlpit Lane.

SEA FIELD, C. 1910. Before Seafield Terrace was built the land was used as a playing field, and the Sea Field was the site for many sports and celebrations. By the time of this picture the field was used by a local farmer, and cows are grazing on land which is now the site of the bowling green.

QUEEN STREET, SEATON, C. 1908. A farmhouse called Lowman's Farm once stood at the junction of Beer Road with Queen Street. The farmyard was where the SWEB showroom now stands but, by the time of this photograph, the farm had gone, to be replaced by a house called Ridgeway, occupied by John Kingsbury Hole. Frank Thomas ran a dairy on the corner of Cross Street, and the premises are still called Thomas' Dairy.

THE REGAL CINEMA, SEATON. This cinema, which opened in 1938 and stood on the present Windsor Gardens, provided family entertainment for the town until its closure in 1972. Going to the pictures was a favourite form of family outing, and when the Regal first opened you could have refreshments in the upstairs tea lounge. Saturday mornings were reserved for the children, usually with a programme of westerns and Disney. The cheers from the children were plainly audible outside.

DEMOLITION OF THE REGAL CINEMA, SEATON, c. 1975. The closure and subsequent demolition of the Regal Cinema caused much feeling in the town. The 'Save the Seaton Cinema Campaign' resulted in a petition signed by 2,544 people. Car stickers appeared all over the town and at that time the closure of the cinema seemed to be on everyone's lips.

TOM CLARK'S BLACKSMITH WORK SHOP, Stock Lane, Seaton, c. 1959. Tom Clark, and his father before him, ran a blacksmith's business from this yard for many years. Up until 1950 it was a common sight to see horses waiting in Stock Lane to be shod, and many of the fine ornamental iron gates to be seen in East Devon were made by Tom Clark in this yard.

TREVETT'S FILLING STATION AND GARAGE, Harbour Road, Seaton, c. 1958. This filling station, which stood on the site of what is now the Rainbow gift shop, was built in 1935 on the old Burrow Field. The first owner was Mr A.E. Good and it was occupied by the army during the Second World War. The filling station was bought by George Trevett during the late 1940s.

LOOKING DOWN QUEEN STREET, SEATON, 1897. The shop on the left belonged to J. Real, who was a tea dealer, poulterer, greengrocer and dealer in rabbits.

SITTING ON THE SIDMOUTH ESPLANADE WALL, Mr James, a visitor from Luppitt, poses for his photograph with the local ice-cream man. The tall building in the background was then Trump's Café.

FORE STREET, SIDMOUTH, c. 1901. The omnibus office of J. Lake and Son can be seen to the right of this photograph. The Lakes owned a livery establishment, and the people standing outside their booking office could have been waiting for the horse-drawn station bus. Opposite the omnibus office was a dairy run by Mr C.A. Maeer. The family grocer business of Trumps is obscured by the horse-drawn coach.

PAUNTLEY LODGE, SIDMOUTH, c. 1908. This lodge was presented to Sidmouth by Lord Hambleden, the owner, after the Second World War, making the Lodge the most picturesque council house in the country. Pauntley itself, a Georgian house in Cotmaton Road, was originally named The Marino. The house was renamed Pauntley in 1923 and during the Second World War was taken over by evacuees from the East End of London.

SIDFORD PACKHORSE BRIDGE, 1868. Fortunately the old packhorse bridge at Sidford was preserved when the road was widened in 1930.

SECTION TWO

The Villages

ROCK FARM, BEER, C. 1918. Three children pose to have their photograph taken in Townsend, Beer. The village was known for Honiton lace, and Beer had the honour of making the lace which adorned the bridal gown of Queen Victoria. While the women of the village were thus engaged most of the men earned their livelihood by fishing, agriculture or the quarrying of Beer stone. Beer itself was, and still is, a most picturesque village, fortunate in escaping the development that was ruined so much of the Axe Valley.

GULLY SHOOT, COLYFORD, C. 1900. The area at the bottom of Gully Shoot was known as Bishops Stoke and Mr Board lived in one of the cottages on the left at this time. Board had a local fish round and herring could be purchased from him for as little as 1s. a dozen.

THE OLD WHEELWRIGHT'S HOUSE AND WORKSHOP, Colyford, c. 1937. The wheelwright at the beginning of the century was Dick Langford, who used to think nothing of walking into Exeter in his younger days, before public transport was available. The house later became a café, selling teas and coffees, and then a public house in the 1970s.

BELMONT TERRACE, BEER, c. 1912.

ST MICHAEL'S CHURCH, BEER, c. 1885. The foundation stone was laid on 26 April 1876. The church replaced a chapel of rest attached to Seaton parish church. The shop to the left of the church later became a cottage, and was pulled down to make way for the Mariners' Hall. The house in the foreground has a sign which reads: 'Local Constabulary', so this must have been the residence of the local policeman.

LOOKING DOWN FORE STREET, BEER, c. 1885. The thatched cottages on the right were pulled down to make way for Beach House.

LOOKING TOWARDS BEER CHURCH, 1890. The cottages and barns in the foreground, bordered on the Meadows, are now demolished.

GENERAL VIEW OF BEER, c. 1907. Although Beer is famous for Honiton lace and its fishermen, another industry, once flourishing but now obsolete, was the making of gun flints. Before the invention of the percussion cap, many thousands of gun flints were made every year out of dark flints embedded in the chalk cliffs, and local manufacturers had large government contracts for the army and navy.

THE DOLPHIN HOTEL, BEER, c. 1905. The section of the Dolphin on the right of the picture was built as a farmhouse, and is one of the oldest buildings in the village. This farm had six tied cottages for its workmen, and land that went half-way to Branscombe.

THATCHED COTTAGES AT SWAN HILL, COLYFORD, C. 1910. The increase in traffic made it necessary to widen the road at the top of Swan Hill. These cottages lost part of their front gardens in the process. Colyford itself was once a town of some importance but its civic glories have faded. It does, however, remain a Borough with a fifteenth-century mace. The profits from the annual fair used to belong by right to the mayor, but these days the profits from the Goose Fayre are distributed to benefit the village and local organizations.

MEET AT THE WHITE HART, COLYFORD, C. 1899. Close to the White Hart and not far from the Axe Bridge is a meadow known as Chantry Meadow. This was endowed to the chantry of St Edmund's chapel near Colyford Bridge, and was mentioned in the Chantry Roll of 1547.

GORDON TERRACE, CLAPPS LANE, BEER, c. 1905.

BEER FISHERMEN compete for the best decorated boat in the 1924 regatta.

MR FRANK WOODROW, BRANSCOMBE, c. 1954. One of the Branscombe cliff farmers, Frank Woodrow grew early potatoes on the steep local hills, with their gradients of 1 in 7. He tackled this job for over sixty years, using donkeys to carry the panniers with 135 lb of potatoes in each, and hand tools of the same design as those his forefathers used. With him in this photograph are his three grandchildren, left to right: Andrew Woodrow, Maureen Woodrow and Geoffrey Gratton.

COLLECTING SEAWEED FROM BRANSCOMBE BEACH, c. 1939. The little plots on the steep, sheltered slope of the cliffs which produced the famous early potatoes were manured with seaweed from the beach. Frank Woodrow, pictured here on the right with son-in-law George Gratton, is collecting the seaweed to be carried away on the backs of two donkeys.

THE PARISH CHURCH OF ST WINIFRED, BRANSCOMBE, c. 1904. The church, an ancient building of stone, is dedicated to St Winifred, a virgin martyr of seventh-century Wales. The main part of the fabric is late Norman and a brass tablet in the tower records the vicars of Branscombe. At the time of this photograph, the living was held by the Revd Robert Swansborough.

BRANSCOMBE SQUARE, c. 1890. The thatched cottage in the foreground was replaced by a house, now named Eland.

OLD CHURCH, BEER, C. 1865. This old church, situated at Beer, was the chapel of rest for Seaton parish church. Until 1905 Seaton and Beer were attended by the same vicar. The nave of the chapel dated from Norman times, although the aisle was Perpendicular, dating from the fifteenth century. The church was pulled down in 1875 and replaced by the present St Michael's.

THE ANCHOR HOTEL, BEER, C. 1899. The monument standing on the plot in front of the Anchor Hotel commemorates Hamilton Macallum, the artist, who for many years made Beer his home. When he died in 1896, at the age of 55, this memorial and stone seat were erected by his friends. The thatched cottages next to The Anchor were pulled down and the site is now the car park.

COURT HALL, SIDBURY, C. 1875. Court Hall, which dates from the late sixteenth century, got its name from the time when the judges stayed there on their circuit rounds.

THREE HORSESHOES INN on the main Seaton to Sidmouth Road, c. 1908. Close by the Three Horseshoes is a monument to a Thomas Gilbart Smith MD, FRCP who, after watching the glorious sunset of 3 August 1902, fell dead from his bicycle.

SHEPHERD'S COTTAGE, BEER, and the brook, c. 1909. The open stream flowing down one side of the main street is known as Beer Brook. This brook, supplied with water from a spring near Bovey House, has never been known to run dry, and no local-born boy worth his salt can be called a Beer boy until he has fallen into it. One of the conduits, made from Beer stone, is pictured here, and these were supplied by the villagers to draw water.

LOOKING TOWARDS ST MICHAEL'S CHURCH, BEER, c. 1900. A contemporary writer said that the Beer cottage folk were kindly and friendly and soft of accent. 'The language of Beer is not to be understood by the stranger, so full of peculiar words and phrases is it. Strange names are read over the shops – the alien lace makers still live, in their descendants, in this corner of the west.' Much has changed since then, but Beer itself remains an unspoilt Devon village.

BEEHIVE COTTAGE, BRANSCOMBE, C. 1895. At this time the cottage was the home of the Collins family.

BRANSCOMBE BEACH, C. 1895. The derelict building at Branscombe mouth had been used to store the culm brought by sea from South Wales to fuel the limekilns on the cliffs, but by the time of this picture it symbolized a vanished industry.

GARAGE AT THE SQUARE, BRANSCOMBE, C. 1938. Frank Dowell owned the first garage in Branscombe, which was built in the 1920s. Nobby Clark, a driver from the garage, recalls that when he came home from a dance at 2 a.m. he was still expected to wash his car in the brook adjoining the garage. Members of the staff included, left to right: Levi Broomfield, Nobby Clark, Frank Dowell (proprietor), Wilfred Salter, Jim White.

BRANSCOMBE LOOKING DOWN TO THE SMITHY, C. 1890. After 100 years the smithy is still there, and today the village blacksmith tradition is carried on by Lyn Bagwell.

CLIFF-SIDE POTATO FIELDS, BRANSCOMBE, c. 1910. The Branscombe cliffs sheltered these plots from the cold winds, enabling the cliff farmers to grow the earliest potatoes in the country.

GENERAL VIEW OF BRANSCOMBE VILLAGE, c. 1895. At this date Branscombe, a long and straggling village, had a population of about 900. The valley in which it lies is still picturesque and beautifully wooded. In this picture you can see the sign for the Masons Arms quite plainly in the right foreground.

BEACH HOUSE, BEER, c. 1904. James Perkins, the builder who lived in Colebrook House, advertised Beach House to be sold or let at this date, with the suggestion that the house would be suitable for a lodging or refreshment house. The cottages on the left were pulled down in about 1918, to become the site of a car park, and Beach House became a hotel.

GENERAL VIEW OF BEER, c. 1899. At this time the native fishermen of Beer were among the most skilful sailors to be found in Britain. There was a legend, which met with general acceptance, that in the seventeenth century a Spanish vessel was wrecked on the rocks in Beer just after the village had been depopulated by the plague. Therefore, the Spaniards, instead of being butchered, were invited to stay and marry the women, thus explaining the swarthiness and seamanship of the Beer fishermen of this period.

TOWNSEND, BEER, c. 1905. The village of Beer is in two parts: the lower village, near the beach, and the top part, known as 'Townsend'. They are connected by the Causeway, where the original Tudor manor house, Starre House, stands.

LOOKING UP FORE STREET, BEER, c. 1900. The tall steeple of St Michael's church on the right hand side of the photograph was taken down several years ago when it became unsafe, partly due to a landmine exploding in the sea off Beer during the Second World War, but also after being struck by lightning after the war. On the left is the Congregational church, which was for some time the sister church to Seaton and was the older of the two churches.

LOOKING TOWARD BANK, BRANSCOMBE, July 1876. The village streets at that time were not made up and were unlit; the average rural cottage was liable to be damp, inconvenient and labour-making. Yet country life, surrounded by open space, was considered far better than life in over-crowded towns.

GENERAL VIEW OF BRANSCOMBE, c. 1905.

High Days and Events

CROWNING OF THE BRANSCOMBE APPLE PIE FAYRE QUEEN, c. 1952. Apple Pie Fayre was revived by the Branscombe British Legion in the 1940s. The apple pies were cooked by Gerald and Stuart Collier in 2 ft squares and in this picture you can see committee members and the queen with her attendants. Front row, left to right: Maxine Pike, Sylvia Hawker, Jenny Reid (Apple Pie Fayre Queen) and Pauline Smith.

CELEBRATIONS AT BEER for the opening of the new church. The opening of the new church in 1877 was long remembered by the people of Beer. Luggers were drawn up in the roads with sails set, men were at their post, bands played and banners fluttered everywhere. Arches were built over the main street, inscriptions were plentiful and this one, full of fancy, went so far as to say 'HE LOVETH OUR NATION AND HATH BUILT US A SYNAGOGUE'.

INAUGURATION OF THE NEW GAS WORKS, SEATON, 30 June 1898. The Seaton Gas and Coke Company was formed in January 1864, with a site for the gasworks on land adjoining the present Lyme Bay Holiday Village in Harbour Road. The original gasworks, costing £1,350, was built on a quarter of an acre site but, with the increasing demand, a new gasworks with larger gasometers was built in 1898. The work was entrusted to Henry Alfred Willey, whose firm of gas engineers was based in Exeter. Willey, pictured here, can be seen with other members of the gas company and the Seaton Urban District Council.

SILVER JUBILEE CELEBRATION, THE ESPLANADE, SEATON. In 1935 George V had been on the throne for twenty-five years. The jubilee celebrations held throughout the country were marked by genuine warmth of feeling. Here the people of Seaton listen to a thanksgiving service on the Seaton sea front.

SEATON REGATTA DAY, C. 1907. Regatta day was held on the last Thursday in July and was the major event of East Devon. All the showmen, such as Anderton and Rowlands, Hancocks, and Brewers, brought their fairs, and other entertainers flocked to the town. Hancocks organized sports in the marshes and one of the big events was the one mile race, won on many occasions during this period by Harry Clapp.

PEOPLE OF SEATON pictured at the Great British Empire Exhibition, which took place at Wembley in 1924.

THOMAS CLAPP, the founder of Clapp's Transport, Seaton, is pictured here taking part in the 1919 peace celebrations. The house in the background is Sea Field House, which was demolished by a bomb during the Second World War. The site is now the Jubilee Gardens.

SEATON CHURCH PARADE, C. 1928. Revd R.S. Robinson, the local vicar, is pictured here passing Seafield Terrace, driving an open touring car and heading the local church parade. He is followed by the Seaton Town Band, who are leading the Boy Scouts, Girl Guides and members of the parish church. The man in the white coat, standing on the right, is Mr Burnside, the dentist whose surgery was in Seafield Terrace.

LAYING THE FOUNDATION STONE of the Seaton Congregational church in Cross Street. The foundation stone for the new church was laid on 21 September 1894 by Morton Sparke Esq. JP, of Torquay. The builder was W.J. Taylor. Before the completion of the church the congregation used to meet at a building in Fore Street.

CLAPP'S TRANSPORT, SEATON, C. 1912. The pair of horses and wagonette driven by Harry Clapp is leaving Manor Road for the Lambert Castle races. These races attracted thousands of spectators and Clapp was the last driver with horses to attend after motor coaches replaced the old way of travel.

CHARABANC TRIP TO CHEDDAR CAVES, C. 1921. Pictured here are the Woodrow family from Branscombe on an outing with their friends to Gough Caves, Cheddar. Rear seat, left to right: Fred Lazel, Mrs Lazel, Ethel Abbott. Standing at back: Herman Brunfield, Mark Newton, John Woodrow (with beard). Front row: Win Woodrow, Mr Cook, Gladys Woodrow, Tryphena Woodrow (can just see her hat), Charlie Woodrow, Louisa Woodrow, Frank Woodrow. The driver and the two lady visitors are unknown.

JAMES LEYMAN, the builder responsible for the Highwell Road development, died in 1925 and in this photograph you can see his funeral cortège leaving the road he built.

SEATON REGATTA DAY, c. 1909. Regatta day was always held on the last Thursday in July and was one of the town's 'red letter days'. Excursion trains brought in people from neighbouring towns and villages to enjoy the entertainments. The paddle steamers, the *Duke* and *Duchess of Devonshire*, as they were called, gave trips around the bay for 6d.

THE SIDMOUTH CARNIVAL was revived in 1957 under the able chairmanship of Frank Lock. The first post-war carnival queen, pictured here with her attendants, was Miss Valerie Moore, who was chosen for her sparkling personality.

OPENING OF THE WEST WALK, SEATON, c. 1925. The old West Walk was washed away during a storm in 1915 and was replaced by the present Walk in 1924. The coping stone was laid by the Chairman of Seaton Urban District Council, Mr C.C. Gould JP, in 1924 and at a later date the West Walk was officially opened by Morrison Bell, the local MP. Present at this ceremony were the following members of the council: Mr J.G. Oldridge, Mr A.J. Acland, Mr A.F. Goddard, Mr J.H. Loud, Mr B. Trevett, Mr W.C.J. Gould, Mr W.J. Newton, Mr A.J. Trezise, Brigadier General G.B. Smith, Sir E. Maconochie and the local surveyor, Mr A. Skinner.

SIDMOUTH REGATTA, a decorated float on the Ham, c. 1890.

SIDMOUTH CARNIVAL, 1958. The carnival princess, escorted by the prince, proceeding to the Ham for the crowning ceremony. She was driven by Ted Gosling in a decorated open-top 1924 Bullnose Morris, with an escort of two St John Ambulance men. The Chairman of the Sidmouth Carnival that year was Frank Lock, the proceeds going to the Sidmouth Cottage Hospital and the Angela Home at Tipton.

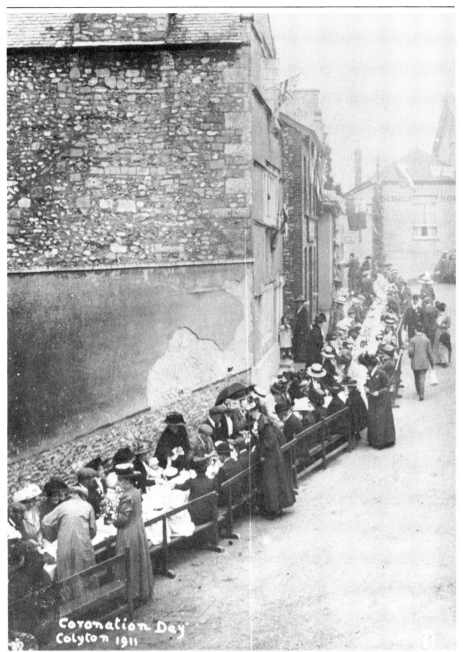

Coronation Day
Colyton 1911

CORONATION DAY CELEBRATIONS AT COLYTON, 1911. The people of Colyton are celebrating the coronation of King George V, sitting in Market Place and enjoying a high tea. Old Church House, on the left, was the home of the Feoffees from 1546 until 1928, and was also the Colyton Grammar School from 1546 until 1927.

CARNIVAL QUEEN, SIDMOUTH, 1958. This photograph was taken at Exeter Carnival, when the Sidmouth Carnival Queen Tableau won the Bruford Cup for the Best Carnival Queen's Tableau in Devon. Pictured here is Elizabeth Vincent and her attendants.

THE NEW SIDMOUTH LIFEBOAT ARRIVES FOR THE LAUNCH in 1885. Making its way down Sidmouth High Street and led by a procession of cyclists is the new lifeboat, the *William and Francis*. This 34 ft long boat was self-righting, and replaced the *Rimmington*. The coxswain of the *William and Francis* from 1901 to 1912 (when the station closed) was Richard Soloman, who was born in 1856. It was during his term as coxswain that the lifeboat made its one and only rescue.

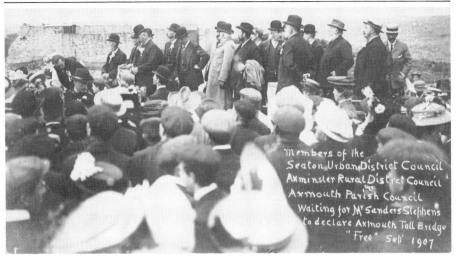

Members of the
Seaton Urban District Council
Axminster Rural District Council
Axmouth Parish Council
Waiting for Mr Sanders Stephens
to declare Axmouth Toll Bridge
"Free" Sep' 1907

CEREMONY TO FREE AXMOUTH TOLL-BRIDGE, 30 September 1907. Members of Seaton Urban District Council, Axminster Rural District Council and Axmouth Parish Council waiting for Mr S. Sanders Stephens to declare Axmouth toll-bridge free. Sanders Stephens contributed £2,000 towards the cost and the ceremony was marked by public rejoicing. The toll bar, together with its supports, was laid out on a huge bonfire and reduced to ashes.

THE END OF THE VICTORIAN ERA and the dawn of the twentieth century. In this photograph, taken in The Square, Seaton on 1 January 1900, the people of Seaton celebrate the new century.

OPENING CEREMONY of Branscombe Wesleyan chapel, C. 1900. The chapel is now a private house.

ROYAL GLEN HOTEL, SIDMOUTH, c. 1887. This splendid four-in-hand with a coach load of passengers must have formed some part of Queen Victoria's Golden Jubilee celebrations in 1887. The Royal Glen was built in 1809 and it was here, just before Christmas 1819, that the Duke and Duchess of Kent stayed with their seven-month-old daughter Victoria, the future Queen. While here, the young Princess had a narrow escape when a boy shooting sparrows in the road outside broke a window with a bullet which narrowly grazed the baby Princess' sleeve.

WISCOMBE PARK HILL CLIMB, C. 1958. Wiscombe Park, between Seaton and Sidmouth, is beautifully situated about one mile from Southleigh. The drive to the house was first used as a hill climb in the 1950s, and the Bugatti pictured here was one of the competing cars.

COMPETITORS AT WISCOMBE PARK HILL CLIMB, C. 1958.

SEATON REGATTA DAY, C. 1906. The motor car on the front belonged to Fred Diment and was the first in the town. Apparently, there was widespread excitement when Fred really gave the car the works and reached speeds of twenty miles per hour.

COLYTON FAIR, HELD AT THE SIDE OF COLCOMBE CASTLE, C. 1896. The auctioneer standing on the steps of Colcombe Castle is selling cattle at the fair which was held in the centre of Colyton.

CELEBRATIONS IN THE TOWN HALL, SEATON. The occasion is unknown, but it must have taken place about 1930. The chairman of Seaton Urban District Council, C.C. Gould, is present, wearing his chain of office. The others are Ben Trevett, Mr Mettam, Mrs Smedley and Jenks White, the local schoolmaster.

EDWARD VII CORONATION CELEBRATIONS in the Burrow, Seaton, c. 1902. Members of Seaton Urban District Council, with other dignitaries of the town, pose to have their photograph taken by George Barton, the town's photographer. Included in this picture are Messrs W.G. Agland, F. Akerman, W.J. Gould, W.H. Head, S. Boalch, H. Thomas, H. Jones, E. Skinner, Mesdames C.C. Gould and Evans and Miss Mayo.

STOKE HILL FOOT BEAGLES MEET AT SEATON, c. 1908. The Beagles hunted hares, and local supporters have gathered to follow the day's sport. The stone building in the background is now R. Dack's workshop and was the only building in Court Lane at that time. Note the elm trees on the right of the photograph; it was never realized how important and characteristic a place in the English countryside the elm tree held until its virtual disappearance through Dutch Elm disease.

STOKE HILL BEAGLES, SEATON, c. 1908. After the meet in the cricket field, the Stoke Hill Beagles, with followers, were going via Colyford Road to the Marshes to hunt hare. Note the sign on the left, advertising Michelin tyres and Trevett's Garage.

SILVER JUBILEE CELEBRATIONS, Fore Street, Seaton, c. 1935. On 6 May 1935 the whole country united to acclaim George V when he celebrated the Silver Jubilee of his reign. There were flags and banners everywhere and in this photograph we can see the extent of the local decorations.

PARTY MENU, CORONATION DAY, SEATON, c. 1911. The coronation of King George V and Queen Mary was held on 22 June 1911 and the people of Seaton enjoyed a day of celebration, followed by a meal in Gould's Temperance Hotel in Station Road.

MAYPOLE DANCING AT GLENMORE, Barline, Beer, 1957. Standing on the right, with her back to the camera, is Miss Beryl Ham, the Beer Primary School mistress. The maypole was a feature of many village activities and Miss Ham taught generations of Beer children the dance.

MEET OF THE AXE VALE HARRIERS at Colcombe Castle, Colyton c. 1930. The Axe Vale Harriers met two days a week to hunt foxes and hares, with a season from the middle of September through to the middle of April.

FREAK WEATHER CONDITIONS AT SEATON, c. 1929. The foam pictured here on Seaton sea front, caused by freak weather conditions, was several feet deep in some parts.

FLOODING OF THE RIVER AXE, 1973. Severe flooding of the River Axe took place in 1973. The man on the left is Alan White, standing next to his chalet where he lived for eleven years. Alan White was born in Beer, the son of John White, a well-known local artist. He joined the Devon Police in 1923 and was a sergeant when he retired in 1948. Mr White died in 1979 aged seventy-seven years.

CELEBRATION DINNER, Everest Drive Self-build Group, Seaton, c. 1954. Everest Drive will always remain a monument to a group of Seaton people who overcame many of the difficulties that existed in post-war Britain and formed one of the first self-build groups in the country. Many of the original group still live in the homes they built nearly forty years ago and the estate, well-kept and cared for, is a tribute to them all. As the houses were finished in 1953, the same year as the conquest of Everest, the road was aptly named. In this photograph, sitting in the front are, from left to right: Mr and Mrs A. Baker, Mr and Mrs Ken Gould and Mr and Mrs Des Garrett. Others include Mr and Mrs F. Cockram, Mr and Mrs G. Clements, Mr and Mrs W. Barnard, Mr and Mrs A. Hayes, Mr and Mrs E. Purse, Mr and Mrs Adams, Mr and Mrs L. Northcott, Mr H. Northcott, Tom Bennett, Mr and Mrs Saxby, Mr and Mrs F. Davis, Mr and Mrs J. Bastone and Joan Otton.

QUEEN VICTORIA'S DIAMOND JUBILEE CELEBRATIONS AT BEER, 1897. Standing in the doorway of their home at No. 1 Gravel Cottage are Lizzie and Bob Boles.

SOME OF THE FIRST FOOTBALL TEAM IN SEATON, outside the George in 1922.

SECTION FOUR

The People

THE AKERMAN FAMILY OF SEATON, 1915. Frank Akerman expanded the family business first founded by his great-grandfather in 1811. He trained as an ironmonger in Bideford, where he met his wife, Marion Boyle. The firm's employees included two tinsmiths who worked on the premises, and later diversification involved a sports and shoe shop. Everything from a 12 bore gun to a copper kettle could be bought here! William (Bill) enlarged the builders merchants division sited in Beer Road (now Tanyards Court) to include plumbing, electrical work, glass cutting and a paint shop. The builders merchants closed after William's premature death in 1951, while the ironmongers continued under a succession of managers, the last being Sid Churchill. In the early 1960s the firm was bought out by Geoff and Betty Rogers, who have been succeeded by their son David. Left to right: Frank Junior (he was killed in action, August 1918 and is buried at Duisans, France), Kitty (who married Jim Smith), Frank Akerman and wife Marion, William (who carried on the family business) and Betty (who later managed the shoe shop at No. 6 Fore Street).

ZENO GOOD, who was born in Seaton in 1838, was the half-brother of Samuel Good, the town's first photographer. Their father, Joseph, built many of the town's fine buildings, including the Castle, Cliff House, Sea Field House and Seaforth Lodge. Zeno, who ran apartments at Cliff House Hotel, is pictured here not long before his death in 1908.

THE TRADING VESSELS THAT SAILED REGULARLY from Axmouth harbour were piloted into the River Axe by a Trinity House pilot. Pictured here, walking down to his home in Queen Street, Seaton, is Isaac Tidbury, the last Trinity House pilot to work in Axmouth harbour.

BILLY MARTIN, AXE VALE HOUNDS KENNELMAN, c. 1926. The Axe Vale Hounds were kennelled then on the present-day private residential site appropriately named Harriers Close. The noise and smell from the kennels didn't matter because, in the early 1920s, the town stopped short of Court Lane.

HAYMAKING IN THE VICARAGE FIELD, SEATON, c. 1909. The present-day Case Gardens were built on the vicarage field, and in this photograph some of the men of Seaton are working at haymaking. Left to right: Long, Newton, Pearce, Real, Peach, Sellars and Chant. The little boy is one of the Peach family.

JACK PEACH, delivery boy for Goulds Bakery, c. 1923. Jack Peach, who was born at Seaton in 1906, left school at fourteen to become a delivery boy for Goulds. He used to assist in the bakehouse and was once told that he was not paid to think after informing his boss that he thought the bread was burning – it burnt. He left the bakery to become an apprentice plumber with Goodings, and started his own plumbing business in 1948. In the early days he cycled to jobs with his tools on the back of his bicycle. Jack Peach, who died in 1981, served for many years in the Seaton Fire Brigade, playing an important part during the German blitz on Plymouth and Exeter in the Second World War.

JACK MIZEN WITH THE BEER TO SEATON BUS, c. 1925. The Pioneer Garage in Beer ran the first bus service between Beer and Seaton and Mizen, pictured here, was one of the first drivers.

THE CLAPP FAMILY were in transport in Seaton for over 100 years. The business started in 1880, with horse-drawn buses plying between the railway station and the town; these were quickly supplemented by a wagonette, a drosky, a brougham, a landeau, a hearse and a four-in-hand brake. The Clapps entered the motor trade in 1921 and ran motor coaches between 1925 and 1935. Horse-drawn vehicles were maintained until 1927 and the riding stables closed in 1948. The three generations of the family who ran the firm are pictured here. Thomas, the founder of the firm, is sitting on the chair, with his son Harry standing behind him. Harry's grandson Geoffrey is sitting on Thomas' knee. Geoff Clapp, who died in 1990 aged seventy-nine years, was the last member of the family in the business.

SEATON TOWN FOOTBALL TEAM, St James' Park, Exeter. In 1953 the Seaton Town First Team were in the Football Express final. They played at St James' Park, Exeter against Silverton and lost 2–0. From left to right, standing: Don Rodgers, Jim Taylor, Alan Hayes, Ken White, Len Pritchard. Front row, left to right: Ivor Anning, Cyril Rodgers, Ron Anning, John Collins, Jim Anning, Bunny White. Seaton team mascot in front: Roy Hutchings.

SEATON MIXED HOCKEY TEAM at an away match during the 1931/2 season. From left to right, standing: Harry Leyman (his father was responsible for the York Road and Highwell Road development), Geoffrey Clapp (who owned Clapp's Garage), Tony Ratcliffe (a first class cellist and local dance band leader), George Trevett (who owned Trevett's Garage in Harbour Road), Lou Poore (a bank clerk at the Midland), Teddy Haslop (a self employed electrician). The ladies sitting in the front include Phyllis Richards, Evelyn Price and Kathleen David.

DR ARTHUR SMART at a Seaton Camera Club Exhibition, c. 1970. Dr Smart, pictured here, was born in 1895. Educated at Rugby School and Cambridge University, he came to Seaton in 1923 and lived at Netherhayes, Fore Street, where he practised medicine for twenty-seven years before moving to Withylake, Seaton Down Hill in 1950. He became senior partner in the practice and retired in 1959. During the First World War he was ship's doctor on HMS *Cyclops* and was wounded in the Battle of Jutland. Dr Smart came from a medical family, his father having practised in Warwickshire and his grandfather, Sir William Stuart, having been a leading surgeon in the Royal Navy. His spare time interests included bird-watching and photography. As a member of the camera club, he was an accomplished colour photographer. In the 1920s he was developing his own black-and-white plates in his darkroom at Netherhayes. During his years in Seaton, Dr Smart was a much loved and respected man.

WALT PEACH, C. 1938. Mr Peach, who lived in Manor Cottages, Seaton, was one of those people, so few and far between today, who took a tremendous pride in his job. The cart-horse pictured here, well-groomed and with shining brasses, belonged to Seaton Urban District Council where Peach was employed for many years.

JOHN GOSLING. John was born in Colyton in 1866 and is pictured here with three of the indoor staff of Halsdon House near Honiton, where he was head gardener. He died in Seaton in 1945.

DELIA SWEETLAND. Mrs Delia Sweetland, who died in Colyton in 1924, was a woman of keen intellect, but of a stubborn disposition which often bordered on the eccentric. On her death she left remarkable instructions concerning her burial. She requested that her heart be pierced and her head severed from her body in the presence of three doctors, and that her remains be cremated. This was all carried out under the direction of her medical adviser, Doctor Langan of Axminster.

BRANSCOMBE VILLAGE SCHOOL, C. 1925. Back row, left to right: Gladys Pike (in black), Gwyneth Abbott, Win Woodrow, Ralph Salter, Gerald Abbott, Eric Dewer, Cyril Evans, Vernon Wyatt, Ada Ward, Gertrude Gosling, Elsie Warren (in boots). Middle row: -?-, Dulcie Wyatt, Ruth Salter, Gladys Woodrow, Dorothy Gosling, Alma Ward, -?-, Phyllis Lugg. Front row: Allan Gosling, -?-, Clarence Evans, Bertie Warren, Oscar Pike, Master Dewer.

BILL HUTCHINGS AND HAYRAKE, SEATON, c. 1930.

HAYMAKING IN THE SEA FIELD, SEATON. Before the present day bowling green was opened in 1929, the Sea Field was use for making hay. Harvest time pictures are always attractive, but in reality the traditional method of gathering and storing hay was laborious. Cut with a horse-drawn mower and loaded onto the wagons with pitchforks, the hay was then stacked by hand into ricks. The work was extremely hard, but most of the men sang or whistled as they laboured and each one took great pride in his work.

MR C.F. GOSNEY AND FAMILY MEMBERS, C. 1901. Gosney ran the town's chemist shop in Marine Place, Seaton until his death in 1935. He was famous for his home-made medicines, such as Gosney's Neuralgic Mixture, Gosney's Bronchial Syrup and Gosney's Corn Cure which reputedly cured corns within a few applications. You get the impression from his early advertisements that, if you had it, Gosney could cure it. One of his two daughters was Eileen Gosney, who died in 1988 after devoting her life to researching the history of her native town. She was a founder member of the Axe Valley Heritage Museum.

SEATON RUGBY FOOTBALL CLUB, 1894/5. This highly successful club produced one player who was capped for the county and became first reserve for the England team. Back row, left to right: H. Evans, C. Real, G. Rodgers, Fred Trinnemen, Ern Tolman, Jess Hooper, Fred Pearce, Harry Jones. Front row: Jack Jones, Sammy Rodgers, Dr Monty May, Ern Collins, Billy Head, Fred Abbott, Bill Real, Tom Harding, Dan Searle.

JAMES WILLIAM SKINNER and his wife Sarah are pictured here in 1899 with their daughter Ada Louise at the rear of Salcombe House, Seaton. The Skinner family had lived in Seaton since the eighteenth century, and the family patriarch was Richard Skinner. Richard, who was born in Seaton in 1779 and died in 1860, was James' father. He was a man of many accomplishments and must have been a wonderful character. He was a mariner and a coal merchant and travelled the world, even sailing as far as China. James, who died in 1913 aged 87, lived at Salcombe House and ran a bakery business from there. He was also the owner of the Golden Lion inn. Daughter Ada never married and died in 1945 aged 87.

SEATON FOOTBALL CLUB, c. 1951. Back row, left to right: Bunny White, A. Baker, S. Price, R. Anning, K. White, L. Pritchard. Front row: R. Nash, D. Garrett, D. Real, A. Crichard, J. Anning.

BRANSCOMBE FOOTBALL TEAM, c. 1954. Back row, left to right: John Andrews, Ralph Salter, Dave Loynd, Eddie Collins, Dereck Loynd, -?-. Front row: Derek Stephens, -?-, George Grattan, Tom White, Chris Andrews.

FRANK WOODROW OF BRANSCOMBE. Frank, who died in 1971 aged eighty-four years, was one of the last cliff farmers in Branscombe who grew early potatoes. Pictured here with his horse Topsy, he was still working until three years before his death. Before the First World War he was a local carter and one of his jobs included the collection of bodies of local people who had died in Exeter hospital. Passing through Sidford, people would often stop him as he was carrying the coffins and say, 'Make sure he doesn't jump out and beat you up Trow Hill, Frank.'

OUTSIDE BRANSCOMBE CHAPEL, c. 1925. Pictured here is Miss Marjorie Loveridge, who was a fine singer and sang on the radio. She was reputed to have had the first car in Branscombe. The girls were dressed in national costumes to commemorate World Christianity. Left to right: Gwyneth Abbott, Lena Cox, Rita Abbott, Win Clarke, Betina Collins, Marjorie Loveridge (daughter of the village blacksmith).

SEATON GOSPEL HALL SUNDAY SCHOOL OUTING, c. 1930. Taking part in the fancy dress race are back row, left to right: Joe Anning, Ben Turner, Albert Anning, John Gosling, Alf Laurence. Front row, left to right: Art Turner, Sydney Ferris, Herman Anning.

SEATON CARNIVAL COMMITTEE, c. 1951. The Seaton Carnival was jointly run by the Seaton British Legion and the supporters of the Seaton Town Football Club. The committee seem to have had some big attractions in those days. The Jolly Waggoners, who were playing their square dance music at the Town Hall, played regularly on the BBC and had a wide following. Left to right: Ted Gosling, Tommy Beaven, Harold Northcott, Mrs H. Northcott, F. Beedon and Jack Hales.

SEATON TOWN BAND, c. 1904. The bandmaster at that time was Mr James, pictured here on the right of the photograph, wearing a braided uniform. Other members of this band included Harry Clapp, Albert Hooper, Tom Rodgers, Jack Beer, Henry Giles and Bill Robins.

SEATONIANS HAYMAKING, 1928. This photograph was taken in Lake's Field. This is now the site of houses on the north side of Highwell Road, to the back entrance of Ryalls Court. From left to right: Jack Lake, John Gosling, Bill Whatley, John Pengelley.

BEER STONE QUARRIES, c. 1900. The huge block of Beer stone loaded on the wagon drawn by four horses is leaving the quarry for Seaton station. The facilities provided by the railway at that time allowed the stone to be easily transported to distant places, thus creating a greater demand. In the past the quarry had supplied material for many Devon churches, including much of Exeter Cathedral.

GRAPEVINE TERRACE, BRANSCOMBE, c. 1920. A group of Branscombe villagers are making Honiton pillow laces. Left to right: Charlie Woodrow, Frank Woodrow, John Woodrow, Tryphena Woodrow, Mini Northcott, Mrs Summers, Lena Cox.

HIGH STREET, SIDMOUTH, C. 1935. Nobby Clarke, shown here, worked for Harry Halford. He started work at 5 a.m., when he picked up the milk from the farm near the Blue Bell Inn, Sidford. At Christmas time Nobby was given a double rum to see him on his way. Clarke can be seen here delivering his milk in a can, from which he poured it straight into the customer's jug.

COLYTON PRIMARY SCHOOL, C. 1954. Several Branscombe children shown in this photograph were taken by bus daily to Colyton Primary School.

A MORRIS COWLEY FOR SIXPENCE – Seaton hotelier Mr Herbert Arthur Good is pictured here with the car he won in 1933 in a raffle at a Conservative fête at Lord Clinton's seat, Bicton. The draw ticket for the car cost sixpence!

VINTAGE CAR, SEATON SEA FRONT, c. 1957. Pictured here in his 1924 vintage two-seater Bullnose Morris is Ted Gosling. He attended many rallies with this car, including the parade of vehicles at the opening of the new National Motor Museum at Beaulieu. In 1958, at a rally in which over 500 surviving Bullnose Morrises were present, he met Lord Nuffield, the founder of the Morris car factory. The Devon and Exeter Savings Bank in the background is now the Trustee Savings Bank.

THOMAS HENRY STOCKER PULLIN MD, FRCS. Dr Pullin was in practice at Sidmouth for fifty-six years. He had the honour of being presented to His Majesty the King at a levée held at Buckingham Palace on 26 February 1906. He lived in a house in Sidmouth High Street which is now the office of the Bristol and West Building Society. As a boy, Dr Pullin was educated at Christ's Hospital. He was head chorister and sang solo on 9 November 1837 when 'God Save the Queen' was first sung in public. He was among 900 scholars who sang at St Paul's Cathedral, in front of Queen Victoria, on her first visit to the metropolis following her coronation. Dr Pullin was one of the earliest volunteer officers of the Sidmouth Battery of Artillery. This company followed the First Devon Volunteer Company in Exeter in 1852. Dr Pullin was a total abstainer and never smoked in his lifetime.

MAJOR JAMES ALBERT ORCHARD VD. Born in Exeter, Major Orchard became a solicitor in 1880 and was taken into partnership by Mr Radford of Sidmouth. Elected a member of the Urban District Council of Sidmouth in 1896, he was chairman at the first meeting and subsequently became Clerk to the Council. Major Orchard assisted in the formation of the Sidmouth Company of Volunteers and was granted the honorary rank of Major in 1898. He was elected first Honorary Secretary of the Cottage Hospital and became treasurer of the Sidmouth Lodge of Freemasons.

SIDMOUTH CARNIVAL CELEBRATIONS, 1958. Carnival Queen Elizabeth Vincent, dressed as a clown and riding a penny-farthing, is assisting with street collections.

JACK LOUD – THE MILKMAN, 1913. Jack Loud went round from door to door supplying milk from a churn into the customer's jug.

W.L. OBORN. Oborn founded the Townsend Garage of Beer in 1922. Mr Oborn, who died in the 1970s aged eight-two years, is shown sitting in a 1929 Austin.

JIM PEARCE, THE SEATON WHEELWRIGHT, C. 1910. Pearce, pictured here with his staff, had his workshop on the site of the present Seaton Evangelical church. With the disappearance of farm wagons, the wheelwright's craft was sadly lost, together with the class of men who worked with an ability born of long experience.

SEATON GROUP, c. 1895. Although we know the names of this group of Seaton dignitaries pictured by local photographer G.W. Barton, the occasion is unknown. Left to right: Harry Abbott, Harry Jones (the postman), C.J. Gosney (the chemist), J.G. Oldridge (the schoolmaster), Mr Stickland (the bank manager), Samuel Good (the photographer), R. Follett (the store-keeper), W. Badcock (the carter), Parson Beale, Doctor Evans, Parson Richardson.

THE RT HON SIR JOHN HENRY KENNAWAY BT, PC, MP, DL, JP, MP for Honiton Division. Sir John Kennaway was born on 6 June 1837 and was MP for Devonshire (East) between 1870 and 1875, and for Honiton Division from 1885. He was Deputy Lieutenant and Justice of the Peace for the County of Devon. A man of good judgement and vast experience, he was one of the most respected men in East Devon.

THE NEWTON FAMILY. For over 100 years the Newton family were fishermen on Seaton beach, and James Newton, the patriarch of the family, featured in John Trotandot's *Ramblings, Roamings and Recollections*. Members of the family pose in this picture, taken in 1930, with Dick Wilkins. Wilkins, second from left, a wonderful character, was one of the best-known men on the beach until his death in the 1970s. Tom Newton, second from right, won the OBE during the Second World War when he pushed a mine out of the River Axe with an oar.

SEATON SCOUTS IN THE VICARAGE FIELD, c. 1914. The first Boy Scout troop was formed in Seaton during April 1913 and Scouts were sworn in on 5 May 1913. The scoutmaster was A.R. Wyatt and assistant masters were W. Giles and W. Newton. The Revd R.S. Robinson was chaplain and A.G.J. Jackson was secretary. Left to right: -?-, Len Smith, Bill Sutton, Revd Robinson.

ALFRED JAMES PAGE SKINNER, COLYTON CHEMIST. A.J.P. Skinner carried on the business of chemist at Colyton from 1892 to 1929. The shop is still there and still a pharmacy after 100 years. He was the eldest of the four sons of Mr and Mrs James Skinner of Seaton, his brother Ernest being the surveyor to Seaton Urban District Council, and Alfred, a bachelor, died aged 77. He was an authority on genealogy and was responsible for the transcription of the parish registers of Colyton, which date from 1538. He joined the Devonshire Association in 1902 and contributed papers on Southcutt of Dulcis Hayes and Walrond of Bovey. During his time few men had as much experience in transcribing parish registers.

COLYTON PRIMARY SCHOOL, c. 1952.

THE WOODROW FAMILY, BRANSCOMBE. John Woodrow, pictured here with his wife Mary Ann, lived in Grapevine Terrace, Branscombe and died in 1929 aged seventy-four years. John was one of the Branscombe cliff farmers who grew early potatoes, and he worked on the cliffs until the day he died. When he failed to return home after a day's work, his son found him on his beloved cliffs, where he had collapsed from a heart attack. Sitting, left to right: John Woodrow, Mary Ann Woodrow. Standing: Frank Woodrow (son), Tryphena Woodrow (daughter).

ALL SAINTS' SCHOOL, SIDMOUTH, C. 1908. The girls are wearing the traditional white pinafores and the boys lace collars.

ALL SAINTS' SCHOOL, SIDMOUTH, 1908. Back row, left to right: White, Burgoyne, Hucker, Hucker, Pratt, Inch. Middle row: Buttle, Mitchell, Poole, Spencer, Bartlett. Front row: Frank Hill, Percy Darke, Miss Parrot, Vernon Bartlett, Dennis Gress.

HENRY JOHN AKERMAN, 1828–87. Henry, the Seaton postmaster, was the third generation of postmasters from the same family. His grandfather, who originally came from Burton Bradstock, combined postal duties with boat-building; his boat yard was the site of the present Royal Clarence Hotel. Henry's sister married Samuel Good, the Seaton photographer, who took this photograph about 1890. Left to right: Lilian, the youngest daughter (a talented artist and violinist who died unmarried), Frank, the son (who took over the family business in Seaton, having first served an apprenticeship to Tardews Ironmongers of Bideford), Henry's wife Elizabeth, daughter Florence, Henry John Akerman. Henry's daughter Florence married a Norman Capel and went to live in Vancouver. They had four sons, the eldest of whom returned and was later killed in France in the First World War.

CAPTAIN HEATHCOTE in his garden at Colyford, c. 1929.

SEATON AND COLYTON OPERATIC SOCIETY at Seaton Town Hall, c. 1920.

ALL SAINTS' SCHOOL, SIDMOUTH, c. 1855. All Saints' School was built in 1847 to take 226 children and enlarged in 1904 for an additional 60. According to Kelly's Directory of Devonshire for 1910, the average attendance was 150 girls and 100 infants. In the same year Miss Florence Bright was the headmistress and Mrs Elizabeth Morrell was the infant schoolmistress.

HARRY CLAPP outside Colombe Castle Hotel, Colyton, c. 1920.

Fishermen and the Seaside

CREW OF THE SIDMOUTH LIFEBOAT *RIMMINGTON*, 1879. This 33 ft, ten-oared lifeboat was named after its donor, a Mrs Rimmington of Streatham, and launched on 25 September 1869. The first call came on 5 September 1872, when it rescued men from the Guernsey brig *Frederick William*. A second sea rescue was made on the last day of the same year, when the lifeboat took eleven men and boys from the barque *Emmeline* of Bordeaux and landed them on Beer beach. The *Rimmington* was replaced in 1885 by the 34 ft *William and Francis*. The man standing in the centre of this picture, wearing the white hat, was the secretary, and standing to his left is the coxswain, Edward Bartlett.

HENRY ISAAC CARSLAKE BARTLETT, Sidmouth fisherman, c. 1907. Henry Bartlett, known by his nickname 'Gully', was a member of Sidmouth's oldest fishing family, with ancestors in East Devon going back 700 years. At the time of this photograph all the Sidmouth fishermen had their section on the beach and Gully operated his Ladies' Bathing Machines, pictured here opposite the Marine Public House. These bathing machines had two compartments, one for disrobing and a 'wet' section for putting on the costumes. The machine was wheeled down to the sea until the wheels were half submerged, the ladies then went down three steps to stand in the sea. Gully Bartlett was born on 30 August 1840 and died on 4 February 1929, working on his beloved beach until well over eighty years old.

'GULLY' BARTLETT, SIDMOUTH BEACH, C. 1908.

SIDMOUTH FISHERMEN, C. 1887. Sidmouth fishermen mark the occasion of Queen Victoria's golden jubilee with this photograph. Back row, left to right: Turk Cordey, Ruder Pike, Sam Ware, Fred Bartlett, Punch Woolley, Fred Ware, Bill Ware. Front row: Banty Hook, Jim Bartlett, Jack Tapley, George Horn, Charles Soloman, Dick Soloman.

RIVER SID AND ALMA BRIDGE, SIDMOUTH, c. 1936. The Battle of Alma took place on 20 September 1854 during the Crimea War. The news of the victory caused strong feeling in England; 2,000 men were lost in two hours' fighting, including twenty-six officers. The bridge constructed over the River Sid in 1855 was named after this battle. The bridge pictured here is the second one, built in 1900 by the Urban District Council, replacing the original bridge, which was of a poor construction.

THE PARADE AND BEACH AT SIDMOUTH, looking east, c. 1935. In the background is the bold outline of Salcombe Hill. The cliff, the highest on the south coast of Devon, is 540 ft above sea level.

WHITE CLIFF, SEATON, C. 1900. The path in the foreground went down to the beach at Seaton Hole, to the west of Seaforth Lodge on the Old Beer Road. The path was in use until the 1940s, when it fell away during a wet winter. Seaton Hole was the habitat of the bather, and at the time of this photograph a capstan on the beach used to draw the old-fashioned bathing machines clear of the tide. Mixed bathing was permitted and Seaton, by adopting this rule, kept abreast of the times and met the wishes of the visitors.

VISITORS, BEER BEACH, c. 1925. Between the two World Wars, seaside resorts enjoyed a popularity they have not since regained. The low-slung canvas and wooden deckchairs pictured here were essential for anyone who wanted to relax on the beach in comfort.

PICKING THE GRAPES THAT GREW WILD IN BEER, c. 1925. The monks of Sherborne Abbey cultivated the sloping fields that faced south for the production of wine, and the girl pictured here could be picking grapes from vines that survived from that time.

SHIPWRECKED BEER FISHERMEN AT SIDMOUTH. The three Beer fishermen pictured here with their rescuers were in a boat that sank 100 yards from York Steps, Sidmouth on 23 April 1906. The Sidmouth fishermen who saved them were brothers Scummer and Toby Smith, shown here third and fifth from left. The Sidmouth boat was renamed the *Rescuer* after the incident.

HERRING CATCH AT SEATON BEACH, c. 1923. Nobby Snell, pictured here second from the left, played rugby for Devon and became a first reserve for England. The house in the background to the right was destroyed by a bomb in 1943; four residents were killed and one was dug out alive.

JACK LOUD AND DONKEYS, SEATON, c. 1910. A ride across the beach on a docile donkey delighted children and adults alike, and Loud provided donkeys for the visitors. He was a noted wit, and when asked, 'How do you hire a donkey?' would always reply, 'Put a screw beneath the saddle!' His father went by the nickname of 'Cheesey' Loud; he kept cheeses in the small stone barn on the right hand side of Harepath Road, just before Eyewell Green, and delivered throughout East Devon.

SEATON BEACH, 1900. The beach at Seaton is, for the most part, pebbles, but there is often a good stretch of sand at low tide, especially at Seaton Hole. At the time of this photograph over twenty fishing boats operated from the beach and fishing was still a major industry.

THE NEW WEST WALK, SEATON, 1926. The West Walk had just been built when this photograph was taken and was a great improvement to the town. To the right of the shelters you can see one of the automatic chocolate machines where for 1d. you could obtain a bar of Fry's chocolate. The castellated building in the rear is named The Castle and was built by Joseph Good.

SEATON BEACH, c. 1925. The boatmen on the beach were skilled local fishermen. Visitors to Seaton at that time had no difficulty, wind and weather permitting, in going to sea to enjoy a day's fishing, with every chance of picking up a few mackerel or even rock whiting and bass.

WALT PEACH AND YOUNG BATSTONE demolishing the old Esplanade shelter in 1956. This shelter was the second of four that have stood on this site.

SIDMOUTH BEACH, C. 1898. Following a time-honoured right, all the families of Sidmouth fishermen had their own sections of the beach to work. The bathing machines by the sea-shore in the foreground of this photograph belonged to the Woolley family.

CLIFF HOUSE HOTEL belonged to Bonny Good and between the wars many well-known people, including Bernard Doulton of the Royal Doulton factory, stayed here. Doulton, with his wife and family, came for many years, staying for at least two weeks. Some of the guests in 1924 enjoyed a fancy dress party.

EDWARDIAN VISITORS AT SEATON HOLE, C. 1903. It was fashionable for the middle class to travel to Seaton for holidays and to spend as long as a month to six weeks at a time enjoying the sea air. Gwendolene Marsh, pictured here holding the striped parasol, is sitting in a boat with her friends; she was the daughter of a Yeovil solicitor. The Marsh family were typical of the people who found Seaton a peaceful place to visit, with its variety of natural attractions.

STEAMERS LANDING AT SEATON, c. 1898. During the summer season Cosens and Co. Steamers, from Weymouth, made frequent calls at Seaton, giving visitors the opportunity of enjoying trips to Sidmouth, Torquay, Dartmouth and up the 'English Rhine', as the coast trip was then described. Steamers also came up the Channel from Exmouth.

THE PICTURESQUE SHORE OF LADRAM BAY, Sidmouth, 1889.

SEATON, WEST WALK, c. 1910. Standing in the background, the Jubilee clock tower was erected in 1887 to commemorate the jubilee of Queen Victoria. This clock tower, which stands about 50 ft high, cost £200 and was built on a site given to the town by Sir A.W. Trevelyan. Sea Field House, standing in the centre, was at this time occupied by the local Medical Officer of Health, Albert Pattinson MRCS.

BATH HOUSE AND MARINE PLACE, SEATON, c. 1901. Gwen Marsh and members of her family stand on the beach opposite the Bath House. There were three Bath Houses on this site. The first one was washed away in 1832; this, the third, was built in 1847 and pulled down in 1905/6.

SEATON BEACH AND ESPLANDE, LOOKING EAST, c. 1898. During the late Victorian era the Esplanade mirrored most of Seaton's life and provided a parade for the fashionable, especially in the peak holiday months of July and August when the visitors appeared. The large brick building in this picture was the Beach Hotel, the premier hotel of the town. Standing on the Esplanade, this hotel commanded an uninterrupted view of the bay, and is now Whitecliff residential home.

SEATON ESPLANADE, LOOKING EAST, c. 1885. The building on the left of the foreground was the Seaton Coffee Tavern. This Tavern opened daily from 6 a.m. to 10 p.m., serving breakfast, luncheon, dinner and tea, and was very much the social centre of the town. It had an excellent subscription reading room, with a recreation room and bagatelle tables. The manager at that time was John C. Anderson, who organized dances and concerts for visitors and residents alike.

LOOKING UP THE RIVER AXE, 1877. Twenty years before this photograph was taken the estuary was busy, two schooners plying regularly between Axmouth and London. Many other vessels brought in coal and lime, but within a short time of the single line railway reaching Seaton in 1868, the River Axe closed to commercial shipping.

AXMOUTH HARBOUR, SEATON, C. 1925. The long, narrow building was once an old warehouse. Before the coming of the railway, Axmouth Harbour was very busy and a place of no little importance, but by the time of this photograph it had become a quiet backwater. The Stedcombe Estate sold the harbour to Axminster RDC in 1967, ownership passing to East Devon District Council in 1974.

MR W.H. HEAD AND THE CREW OF HIS BOAT *GRACE DARLING*, c. 1906. William Henry Head, who was born in 1874 and died in 1958, was well-known and, in his time, probably the most popular man in Seaton. He was much involved in the local community, and became Seaton's youngest ever town councillor. The Head family had lived in Seaton since 1607 and owned considerable property in the town. William Henry Head succeeded to the Head estate and lived at The Wessiters. Head is pictured here in his sailing boat *Grace Darling*, with his crew who were members of the Newton family.

CREW OF THE *LADYBIRD*, BEER, c. 1899. The main event in the Seaton and Beer Regatta was the race between the *Ladybird* and the *Grace Darling*. *Ladybird*, owned by Captain Moore, had a crew of Beer fishermen and *Grace Darling*, owned by Billy Head, was crewed by Seaton fishermen. Great rivalry existed between the two owners and the race was the sporting event of the year.

LANDING PASSENGERS AT SEATON, c. 1898. These steamers called frequently through the summer months, and it was possible at that time to enjoy very fine coastal trips east or west of Seaton. Although the town did not boast a pier, the boats carried a landing stage by which means the passengers came ashore with ease and safety.

THE ESPLANADE, SEATON, c. 1895. There was no traffic problem when this picture was taken nearly 100 years ago. The building on the site now occupied by the roundabout was the Bath House, where people used to take remedial hot baths. Inside the Bath House there was a pump which sucked up sea water for the baths. At the time this photograph was taken the Bath House was run by the Vincent family.

SEATON FISHERMEN, 1925. Before the 1920s Seaton fishermen caught mackerel and herring in shoals. They kept three large boats, which were rowed by four men, with a huge net in each boat. The nets were pulled on the beach with the catches of thousands of fish. Mr G. Mutter, the fishmonger, purchased the fish and they were sent in boxes via Seaton station to large towns. However, by 1925 the local fishing industry was already failing, partly due to the sudden disappearance of the herring, the main source of income in the winter. In this picture are members of the well-known local fishing families of Newton and Wilkins.

BEER FISHERMEN, C. 1897. Left to right: Albert Rowe, Mick Aplin, Jim Chapple, Smut or G.
Chapple, Ned Marshall, Ern Miller, W. Woodgate, Thomas Woodgate.

THREE-MAST FISHING LUGGER, BEER BEACH, August, 1877. The Beer fishing boat, a clinker-built craft, was ideal for the job. Constructed of elm on oak frames, the boats were built in the village, with sailing qualities known far and wide. The sails on these boats were made by the fishermen and their families and barked with Burma Cutch to preserve the canvas. In this photograph, the three-mast Beer lugger beached broadside on, with full tackle on board, is waiting to go to sea. The sheltered position of the beach allowed fishermen from Beer to put to sea when others from Seaton and Sidmouth were weather-bound, giving them the reputation of unsurpassed seamanship.

SEATON SEA FRONT LOOKING TOWARDS THE WEST WALK, c. 1962. Taken during the holiday season, before the days of the sea-wall.

ESPLANADE, SEATON, LOOKING WEST, c. 1962. The kiosk to the right of this picture was the booking office for Dove Coaches, who ran trips to many Devon beauty spots.

AERIAL VIEW OF BEER, c. 1930. The Jubilee Gardens to the right of this photograph were laid out in commemoration of the diamond jubilee of Queen Victoria. The gardens open out onto a cliff path by which you can reach the beach. The fishing families of Driver, Aplin and Chapple ran most of the holiday beach attractions, and twenty-four trawlers and eight crabbers were employed in the fishing industry.

BEER BEACH, C. 1896. The beach was a very busy place, with fishing boats packed from one end to the other, the local fishing industry was at its peak and the seamanship of Beer men well-known.

SEATON BEACH, C. 1885. At this date, fishing was a major industry in the town. The fishermen included characters such as Nipper Newton, G. Welch, Abraham Tidbury, Jim Wilkins, Jacob Rowland, Tim Gosling, Billy Power Benham, Jim Taylor, Sam Searle, Jim Newton, Jimmy Jones, Jack Hooper, Tommy Clarke, Tim Hooper, Charlie Driver and Tippy Sam Newton. Hardy men, full of anecdote, they could tell many stories about the sea, weaving romantic tales about Jack Rattenbury and other smugglers. Descendants of these fishermen still live in the town today.

AERIAL VIEW OF SEATON, 17 July 1933, taken by one of the planes from HM Aircraft Carrier *Furious*. Note the absence of any buildings between White Cliff and the Esplanade. At that time there was no New Beer Road and people wishing to travel to Beer used the Old Road. The cliff erosion which has taken place during the past sixty years can be plainly seen. The Grove was then a private house and the adjoining car park was gardens.

The War Years

SEATON ARMY CADET FORCE, c. 1947. Members shown here include Mr Bunny, R. Richards, D. Clements, S. Sluggett, E. Cockram and A. Real.

THE 'V' CAFE AND TEA GARDENS, HAREPATH ROAD, SEATON, c. 1951. This café was built at the end of the Second World War by the Dickens family, who ran the business for many years. At a later date, with a change of owners, the thatch was replaced with tiles, and the café enlarged and renamed the Long House.

NESTLE MUNITIONS FACTORY, BRANS-COMBE, c. 1943. The factory van driver, Jim White, is pictured here loading up shell fuses for delivery to Seaton station.

W.L. OBORN, PROPRIETOR OF TOWNSEND GARAGE, BEER. Oborn is pictured here with an Army bomb disposal squad. The unexploded bomb was dropped by a German bomber in May 1944 in Paizen Lane, Beer.

SOME YEARS BEFORE THE FIRST WORLD WAR a Royal Navy torpedo went astray and came up on the beach at Culverhole Point between Seaton and Rousdon. A navy team went there to attend to it, and Mr G.H. Richards, the Seaton builder, was contracted to convey it to Seaton Hole, where the navy could get it back aboard a vessel. This picture, with Richards third from the left behind the horse, shows the party about to leave Culverhole Point. The charge for the job, including danger money, was £3.

MACHINERY FOR THE NESTLE FACTORY, BRANSCOMBE, c. 1940. With the outbreak of the Second World War, Sydney Pritchard and his brother William won a contract to produce shell fuses and aircraft components. Their factory in Holloway, North London was moved to the garage in The Square, Branscombe. Pictured here on the back of a low-loader, some of the large electric motors are arriving at the factory.

BRITISH LEGION OFFICIALS, c. 1952. Revd H.R. Cooke MC was the chairman of the Seaton branch of the British Legion, and is pictured here discussing the lease of the local branch's new headquarters in the Regal Cinema with colleagues. From left to right: Reverend H.R. Cooke, E.S. Gosling (secretary), A. Gardner (vice-chairman).

DECLARATION OF THE FIRST WORLD WAR, COLYTON, 1914. When England declared war on Germany on 4 August 1914, large and excited crowds gathered in the streets of all towns for news. In this picture, the people of Colyton assemble in Market Square, anxious for information.

REGINALD WILKIE GOSNEY AND HIS SISTER, c. 1905. Reginald, the son of a Seaton chemist, became a second lieutenant of the 76th Punjabis. He was mentioned in despatches in January 1916 and killed in action later the same year.

MEMBERS OF THE NATIONAL FIRE SERVICE, SEATON, c. 1943. During the Second World War, local fire brigades were consolidated into a single National Fire Service, giving the advantage of greater mobility and a universal standard of training and equipment. The firemen pictured here played a heroic part in the defence of Exeter and Plymouth against enemy bombing.

VICTORY CELEBRATIONS, HIGHWELL ROAD, c. 1945. This street party, held in Highwell Road, was to celebrate victory in Europe. Standing on the left is the Seaton vicar, Revd H.R. Cooke MC, who would have paid a visit to the many street parties held on that day.

PEACE CELEBRATIONS HELD ON THE BURROW, SEATON c. 1919. The Great War had ended on 11 November 1918. Over 200 men from Seaton had served and, of these, twenty-four made the supreme sacrifice. The names of these brave men were recorded on the Memorial Cross, which stands at the parish church entrance. Peace celebrations were held throughout the country during the summer months of 1919. There was a tremendous atmosphere of excitement and elation, but the joyous celebrations were for many a time of sadness; these were the mothers and fathers, the wives and the children who knew that their loved ones would never return.

BRITISH LEGION DINNER, ROYAL CLARENCE, SEATON, c. 1952. Back row, left to right: Ern Hussey, Jim Cockram, -?-, Mr Barry, Miss Barry, Mrs W. Hatchley, Mrs J. Real, Walt Ham, Mr Harrison, Miss Harrison. Front row, left to right: Ivy Harris, Miss Barry, Mrs Barry, Mrs J. Cockram, Mrs Edwards, Mrs Franklin, Mrs Tom Newton, Barbara Newton.

PRESENTATION TO THE CZECH ARMY. This photograph was taken in 1943 when Frank Norcombe, Chairman of Seaton Urban District Council, and Francis Garner, Clerk to the Council, visited Dovercourt near Harwich, accompanied by their wives. On this occasion Frank Norcombe attached a ribbon to the colours of the 2nd Battalion of the Czech army who were stationed at Seaton for part of the war. Some of the Czechs returned to Seaton after the war for a visit and were able to renew their acquaintance with Frank.

WILLIAM JOHN BATTEN at the silver jubilee celebrations, Branscombe, c. 1935. Bill Batten was a brave soldier, devout churchman and a friend of all. Founder member of the Branscombe branch of the Royal British Legion, Batten was one of the survivors in the Battle of Bois de Buttes. On 27 May 1918, 850 men of the 2nd Battalion Devonshire Regiment made a last stand at Bois de Buttes. The Germans exacted a heavy toll and only fourteen men survived the battle. This battle is symbolic of the way the Devonshire Regiment fought in Flanders.

TERRITORIALS, SEATON FRONT, August 1914. Behind the regular army and the reservists were the part-timers, the Territorials, men from all backgrounds who left their job for a fortnight's summer camp and attended army drill at least one night a week. These Territorials from Seaton are on parade just after the declaration of war, ready to serve their country.

WAR VETERANS' PARADE at Branscombe silver jubilee celebrations, 1935.

TERRITORIALS, 4TH BATTALION THE DEVONSHIRE REGIMENT, Sidmouth, c. 1936. Nobby Clarke from Branscombe is pictured here, sitting on the right at the end.

NESTLE MUNITIONS FACTORY, BRANSCOMBE, c. 1943. Interior picture of the factory, which had a work force of 114 men and women working day and night in twelve hour shifts. This secret wartime factory at Branscombe turned out millions of shell fuses and aircraft components but was never a target for German bombers. Much credit must go to William and Sydney Pritchard who, with their workers, played an important role in the war effort.

NESTLE MUNITIONS FACTORY, BRANSCOMBE, c. 1943. A team of eleven women inspectors supervised quality control, and in this picture you can see the Admiralty inspection department that checked aircraft components. Morale in the factory was high, with everyone united in a common cause and working hard, encouraged by loudspeakers playing 'music while you work' which, at times, drowned the din of the machines.

SEATON SCOUT BAND, Cross Street, Seaton, c. 1943. The band was playing for the opening ceremony of the Seaton, Colyton, Beer and district 'Wings for Victory Week' on Saturday 22 May 1943. The target for the week was £50,000, which would have bought one Bomber and two Typhoons. Standing to the left of the band is scoutmaster Skipper Brookes.

NAVAL RECRUITS marching up Long Hill, Beer, 3 August 1914. During the previous day these naval reservists would have received a telegram with a one-word message – 'Mobilize.' Hundreds of people lined the road between Seaton and Beer to see them leave by a special train from Seaton station.

BOER WAR PEACE CELEBRATIONS, 1902. Britain entered the twentieth century in the grip of a war which ended in March 1902, and in this picture we can see how the people of Seaton welcomed home their Boer War heroes. Two battalions of the Devonshire Regiment fought in South Africa and were led by General Buller, 'massive, hard-riding, and a paternal squire of the old tradition,' a man who inspired his men with a pride which recalled the days of those Devon sea-dogs, Drake and Hawkins, and despite his differences with authority in London, was always a hero to all true men of Devon. However, to the people of Seaton, this day was for their own local heroes, and they would remember the war and these celebrations for the rest of their lives.

AXMOUTH VILLAGE, 1897. Pictures of this charming village across the river from Seaton will be included in a forthcoming book.

ACKNOWLEDGEMENTS

I am grateful to all those donors who, over the past forty years, have given photographs and postcards to add to my collection. My thanks go to Nobby Clarke of Branscombe for allowing me to use pictures belonging to him. Thanks also to Vernon Bartlett of Sidmouth and Violet Webster of Seaton for loaning material for use in this book. Arthur Chapple of Beer gave much help, and these four people have spoken from their own personal knowledge of times past and a lifetime's interest in their locality. I would also like to thank all those who have contributed valuable information.

Thanks must go to Lyn Marshall, Geoff Marshall, Christine Haworth and Edna Everitt for much appreciated assistance, and to Roy Chapple for patiently answering my questions. I am grateful to my wife, Carol, for her encouragement and help in this book, and to Simon Thraves for his assistance.

The photographs in my collection are now on loan to the Axe Valley Heritage Museum and will one day belong to the town.